A Kid's Guide to
Martial Arts

TAE KWON DO

태권도

Alix Wood

PowerKiDS
press

New York

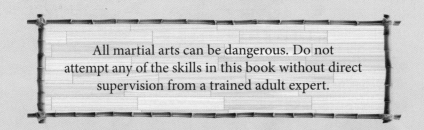

All martial arts can be dangerous. Do not attempt any of the skills in this book without direct supervision from a trained adult expert.

Published in 2013 by Rosen Publishing Group, Inc.
29 East 21st Street, New York, NY 10010

Editor: Sara Antill
Designer: Alix Wood
Consultant: Sandra Beale-Ellis, National Association of Karate and Martial Art Schools (NAKMAS)

With grateful thanks to Finnian Cooling and everyone at Kernow Martial Arts; James, Joshua, and Elaine Latus, Olivia and Dereka Antonio, Solomon Brown, Ryan Fletcher, Alex Gobbitt, Hayden Hambly, Max Keeling, Joshua Nowell, Kyanna and Katie-Marie Orchard, Natasha Shear, Niamh Stephen, Chris Tanner, Jazmine Watkins, and Emily.

Photo Credits: Cover, 1, 6, 14 right, 22, 27, 28 © iStock; 2, 4, 8, 9 bottom right, 11 bottom, 13 bottom left and right, 18 left, 23 © Shutterstock; 5 © Rob Wilson/Shutterstock; 7 © Alain Seguin; all other images © Chris Robbins.

Library of Congress Cataloging-in-Publication Data

Wood, Alix.
  Tae kwon do / by Alix Wood.
      p. cm. — (A kid's guide to martial arts)
  Includes index.
  ISBN 978-1-4777-0316-8 (library binding) — ISBN 978-1-4777-0354-0 (pbk.) —
ISBN 978-1-4777-0355-7 (6-pack)
  1. Tae kwon do—Juvenile literature. I. Title.
  GV1114.9.W66 2013
  796.815'7—dc23
                              2012028710

Manufactured in the United States of America

CPSIA Compliance Information: Batch #WI3PK2: For Further Information contact Rosen Publishing, New York, New York at 1-800-237-9932

Contents

What Is Tae Kwon Do?

Tae kwon do is a Korean martial art and the **national sport** of South Korea. It is well known for its kicking techniques. The Koreans used to think that the hands were too valuable to be used in **combat**.

There are two main branches of tae kwon do, "traditional" and "sport." The traditional branch is tae kwon do as it was done in the 1950s and 1960s, in the South Korean military, schools, and universities. Sport tae kwon do developed after the 1950s. It is divided into two main styles. One is governed by the World Taekwondo Federation (WTF) and the other by the International Taekwon-Do Federation (ITF).

Map showing Korea

THE OLYMPICS

Tae kwon do made its first appearance at the Olympic Games as a demonstration sport at the 1988 Summer Olympics in Seoul, South Korea. In the opening ceremony there was a big demonstration of tae kwon do with hundreds of adults and children performing moves in **unison**.

In Korean, "tae" means "to strike or break with foot" and "kwon" means "to strike or break with fist." "Do" means "way." So, tae kwon do means "the way of the hand and the foot."

You will see tae kwon do written in a number of different ways. It can be "taekwondo" or "taekwon-do," too. The WTF usually uses "taekwondo," while the ITF uses "taekwon-do." Translating the Korean written alphabet into English is done by the sounds the characters make, so there can be a few different accepted versions.

태
Foot

권
Fist

도
Way

Early tae kwon do was a mixture of three unarmed combat styles developed by the three rival Korean kingdoms. The most popular style was taekkyeon. The best taekkyeon students were picked for the special warrior corps, called the Hwarang.

Taekkyeon spread through Korea as the warriors traveled around the country. Over time interest in martial arts faded a little. In 1910 Japan invaded Korea and **occupied** the country for 35 years. Korean martial arts were banned, but the ban made people more interested. Several tae kwon do schools (*kwans*) started up. The nine schools joined together, and the name "tae kwon do" was agreed on.

During the Korean war, the South Korean president watched a performance by martial arts masters. He was impressed when one man broke 13 roof tiles with a single punch. Afterward he ordered his military leaders to make all Korean soldiers train in the martial arts.

The Five Tenets of Tae Kwon Do

Courtesy
Be polite to everyone. Be **courteous** to your instructors and fellow students.

Integrity
Be honest with yourself. Know the difference between right and wrong.

Perseverance
Achieve your goal. Whether it's a higher grade or a new technique, never stop trying.

Self-Control
Be in control of your actions. Live, work, and train within your abilities.

Indomitable Spirit
Show courage when you are in a difficult situation. Never give up.

HWARANG

A tae kwon do **pattern** (set of moves) called "Hwa-Rang" is named in honor of the Hwarang warriors.

Kim Yusin, below, was a Hwarang warrior at age 15. He was a great swordsman and became a leader at 18 years old. He was the most famous of all the generals in the unification wars of the three kingdoms.

A statue of General Kim Yusin at Hwangseong Park in Gyeongju, South Korea

Tae Kwon Do Equipment

To practice tae kwon do safely you may need special clothing and safety equipment. It is best to buy your kit from your club so you make sure you get the right type. At first just wear loose clothing.

A dobok is the uniform worn for Korean martial arts. "Do" means "way" and "bok" means "clothing." The dobok can have a v-neck jacket like the boy below, or a wrap around jacket like the boy on the next page. The dobok can be any color, but white and black are most common.

Sometimes the jacket will have a **logo** of your club on it. So it's important to check with your club before you buy one.

How to tie the belt

1. Place the middle of the belt on your stomach.

2. Pass each end of the belt behind you and back to the front.

3. Cross the right end over the left end.

4. Thread the same end up behind both loops.

5. Cross the left end over the right end. Thread the left end back through the hole to finish the knot.

Everyone starts out as a white belt. A white belt is a 10th "kup" (or "gup") grade student. All the colored belts are kup grades, from 10th to 1st kup until you reach your black belt. Then you are a "dan" or "degree" grade if you are over 16 years, or a "poome" grade if you are under 16.

You may sometimes need to wear protective gear.

9

The Dojang

*The place where you learn tae kwon do is called a **dojang**. The dojang can be a multipurpose hall or a specially-built martial arts school. "Do" means "way" or "path," and "jang" means "place."*

It is very important to respect the dojang. You should stop and bow as you enter. This shows respect to your instructor and respect for tae kwon do. The bow is called a *kyungye* in Korean. Put your feet together and place you hands on the sides of your thighs. Bow smoothly by bending forward at the waist. Dip your head so your eyes look down. In tae kwon do looking at your instructor or partner while you bow shows mistrust, so make sure you always lower your eyes. Count to two and straighten up again.

In some dojangs it is important to stand in the right place. The highest ranked student stands at the front of the class on the right, with the next highest grade on his or her left, and so on. When the front row is full, the next student stands in the second row behind the highest ranked student. So if it's your first class, head to the back left corner of the tae kwon do dojang!

Safety tips

For safety, do not wear a watch or any jewelry. Keep your fingernails and toenails short and tie back long hair with a soft hair tie, not anything metal.

What do you think this girl should do?

Now she is ready to learn tae kwon do safely.

DOJANG FLOOR

Your dojang's floor may be bare or it may have foam mats that sometimes click together like a jigsaw. The mats reduce the **impact** on your joints when you run and jump.

11

Warm-Ups

It is important to warm up before your tae kwon do session. Warming up helps stop you from pulling muscles. If you feel any pain, stop and switch to another exercise or stretch. Don't strain anything.

Neck stretches

Tip your head slowly forward, then back, then to the right, then to the left.

Shoulder stretch

Reach your arms up above your head, cross your hands, and then put your palms together. Hold this position pressing arms backward gently.

Arm circles

Stand with your feet shoulder width apart.

1 Bring both arms up over your head.

2 Circle your arms down and behind you.

3 Bring your arms back up to the starting position.

Shoulder stretches

 Grasp your fingertips and lift one arm so the inside of your elbow is above your head. Hold and then swap elbows.

 Bend one arm down your back and the other arm up your back. Grasp your fingertips and hold. Then swap arms.

The Stances

A **stance** is a way of standing. If your stance is solid, your moves have a strong, stable base. Try making your feet match the drawings. The red line is where your shoulders should be, over your feet.

Ready stance (Chumbi)

1

Stand with your feet shoulder width apart. Cup your hands, palms up, just below belt level.

2

Slowly lift your hands. You are gathering your positive energy. Bring your left foot in next your right foot.

3

Make fists and slowly bring them down level with your belt. Step your left foot out again. Hold your hands away from your body, like the instructor is here.

14

Horse riding stance *(Juchun seogi)*

Horse riding stance is traditionally wide and deep. Some tae kwon do schools do a more upright version. Your feet should face forward, toes slightly inward. Your knees need to be over your toes. Your back should be straight, with your bottom tucked under, not sticking out.

Walking stance *(Ap seogi)*

Walking stance is like normal walking, but your back foot turns out slightly. Keep your back straight.

"GI" OR "CHI"

"**Gi**" means "life energy." It can also be called ki, qi, or chi. It is pronounced "ghee" in Korean. The development of gi is important in many martial arts. **Meditation** makes you mentally ready to perform what seems to be physically impossible.

This symbol is gi written in Korean *hanja*. The top means scholar and the bottom means heart or mind.

Blocks

Blocks are strong moves designed to stop attacks like punches or kicks from hitting your body or head. Tae kwon do blocks have to be fast, strong, and well timed.

Two arms work together to make the block stronger. It's also important that there is a twist on the end of each block. This twist gives the block more power.

Low block

1 Bring your right arm up to protect your face. Your other arm should be out in front of you.

2 Move your blocking arm down to protect your stomach and upper leg. At the same time twist your other arm back to your waist. At first it can be hard to do both arms at once. Try and practice each arm on its own first.

Middle block

1 Bring the blocking arm around to the front strongly, and at the same time bring your other arm in tight to your waist.

2 Bring your blocking arm back with your arm bent and your hand twisted outward. Your other arm protects the chest.

High block

1 High blocks protect your head. The bottom arm is your blocking arm. Hold it at waist height with your other arm up by your chin with palm outward.

TWIST POWER

It's very important that the twist in the hand and **forearm** comes right at the end of the block. This makes the block stronger and more effective.

2 Bring the blocking arm up outside your other arm. Bring your other arm in tight to your waist. Twist both forearms as you move.

17

Strikes

Tae kwon do is the way of the hand and foot. Hand strikes are an important part of tae kwon do. Fancy kicks are great, but if your attacker is at close range, you'll need to use your hands.

A strong, fast, accurate punch is a great weapon. Make your punch go straight to the target. Try punching in front of a mirror at first. Keep your wrist straight or your punch will be weak and you could hurt yourself.

Middle punch

The target area is the **solar plexus**, which is around the bottom of the V-neck on a dobok. As you punch bring your other arm in to your waist.

You should strike with your first two knuckles.

Low and high punch

Use the same technique as for the middle punch, but aim lower or higher.

Back-fist strike

1 The target area is the bridge of the nose. Hold one arm across your body with your striking arm above it and across your shoulder.

2 Pivot your striking arm up and at the same time draw your other hand in to your waist.

MAKING A FIST

Fold your fingertips in tightly, then make a tight fist. Wrap your thumb around the fist. Never put the thumb under your fingers.

Double knife-hand strike

1 Look at your target with your striking hand palm up on your chest and your other hand in a knife hand behind you.

2 Snap your striking hand out, twisting your palm. Bring your other hand to your chest.

MAKING A KNIFE HAND

Press your four fingers together bending the middle finger and ring finger slightly. Leave some space between the forefinger and thumb. Strike with the bottom edge of your hand.

19

Kicks

Tae kwon do is well known for its kicking techniques. The leg is the longest and strongest weapon a martial artist has, so kicks give you the most chance of landing a powerful strike without being hit back.

Once you learn the technique, tae kwon do kicks can be done as jump kicks, spin kicks, jump spin kicks, or multi-rotational spin kicks!

Front kick

To get more power in the kick you need to use your hips, so rotate slightly on your standing foot as you strike.

Your target should be straight in front of you. Lift your knee toward the target.

Drive your foot out by straightening your knee. Strike with the ball of your foot. Bend your knee to bring your foot back.

Ax kick

You need to get your foot above the target to strike downward. Warm up before you try an ax kick. Turn your standing foot out a little as you kick.

1

2

3

Bring your knee up toward your target.

Kick your leg up and then strike with your heel.

Bring your leg back down softly.

Roundhouse kick

1

2

3

Bring your right leg up, keeping your foot as far behind as possible.

Push your leg out and around.

Fully extend your leg and strike with the ball of the foot.

Breaking

Breaking competitions show power, speed, and technique. Competitors break wooden boards of different thicknesses, or several boards stacked one on top of the other.

To progress to a colored belt, tae kwon do students must learn breaking. The breaks you perform get gradually harder. Over time the student's hands and bones get used to breaking boards, and practice hardens the bones, skin, and tendons.

BODY PARTS

In tae kwon do, you can use hands, knuckles, or even fingertips to break boards. Headbutts, knee strikes, elbow strikes, and parts of the foot are also used. As you progress, you move from wooden boards to concrete blocks, like in the picture on the right.

Do not try breaking until your instructor thinks you are ready. It is very easy to hurt yourself. Your instructor will teach you the correct technique and start you with easy boards. You will be taught about how to use the **grain** of the wood, and about what kind of wood is easiest to break. Below is how an advanced student would break a board.

1 Empty your mind and relax. Don't think about success or failure. Take a calming breath. Focus on the target.

2 Focus on a single point. Aim your strike 6 inches (15 cm) beyond the board, not at the board itself. Strike through the target. Concentrate on your speed.

Patterns

Tae kwon do patterns, or poomse, were invented to teach moves to an army. Everyone did the same moves at the same time and practiced them over and over.

The first pattern you learn will probably be *chon ji*. "Chon ji" means "heaven and earth."

⑧ Middle punch

⑦ Lower outer forearm block

⑭ Middle punch

⑬ Middle inner forearm block

④ Middle punch

③ Lower outer forearm block

Start

① Lower outer forearm block

② Middle punch

⑤ Lower outer forearm block

The first part of the pattern represents heaven.

⑥ Middle punch

⑩ Middle punch

⑨ Middle inner forearm block

⑮ Middle inner forearm block

⑪ Middle inner forearm block

⑫ Middle punch

⑲ Middle punch

⑯ Middle punch

⑱ Middle punch

⑰ Middle punch

The second part of the pattern represents earth.

24

Chon ji "Heaven"

Learning a whole poomse can be hard. Try splitting it up into sections and then put it all together once you have learned each part.

Start

Ready stance

1

Lower outer forearm block

2

Middle punch

3

Lower outer forearm block

4

Middle punch

5

Lower outer forearm block

6

Middle punch

STANCE

All the stances in "heaven" are walking stance.

You should be back at the start point after step 4 and after step 8, ready for the second "earth" part of the pattern.

7

Lower outer forearm block

8

Middle punch

25

Sparring

*As soon as your instructor says you are ready you can start **sparring** classes. It might seem frightening at first, but as a white or yellow belt no one will expect you to be perfect.*

A good martial arts instructor will put you against someone who will take care of you first, possibly a black belt. They will increase the difficulty slowly as you improve. Understand that fear is normal and don't let it stand in your way. A good instructor will not put you in danger. Competing is a great way to meet other tae kwon do students. You can see what other people achieve and challenge yourself.

Kicking distance

Learn your kicking distance so you do not miss and waste effort during sparring. Use training pads to help build up your speed, strength, and stamina. Take turns holding the pads for a partner.

FOOTWORK

In tae kwon do sparring, footwork is very important. What happens between your kicks can be more important than the kicks themselves. You will need to learn to slide forward and backward, learn to switch quickly on the spot, and learn to move sideways in a balanced way.

Learn Korean

In tae kwon do, Korean commands are often used. Students may count in Korean during their class, and during tests you could be asked what certain Korean tae kwon do terms mean.

Here are some common parts of the body that may be useful to know.

pahl (arm)   *joomok* (fist)

muh ree (head)

ouka (shoulder)

pahlmahk (forearm)

pahlkup (elbow)

myung chi (solar plexus)

dahree (leg)

mooreup (knee)

bahl (foot or feet)

One of the times you may hear Korean at your dojang is when your instructor is counting.

Counting to 10

English	Korean	English	Korean
one	hana	six	yasut
two	dul	seven	ilgup
three	set	eight	yudol
four	net	nine	ahope
five	dasut	ten	yul

ALPHABET

Korean doesn't have thousands of characters, like Chinese. It actually has a very simple, logical alphabet. There are 14 basic consonants and 10 basic vowels. Letters with similar sounds have similar shapes, so it is easy to learn.

Words you may hear in the dojang

Korean	How to say it	What it means
baro	*BA-ro*	return
charyeot	*CHA-ree-ot*	attention
dora	*DOE-ra*	turn around
guk gi e	*GOOK gie*	face the flags
joonbe	*chune-bee*	ready
ki hap	*KEY hop*	yell
ku mahn	*KOO-man*	stop/break
kyeong ye	*KEE-young-ay*	bow
poomse	*POOM-say*	patterns
shi jak	*SHE-jak*	begin

Glossary

combat (KOM-bat)
Active fighting in a war.

courteous (KUR-tee-us)
Showing respect for and
consideration of others.

dojang (DOH-jang)
A training center for the
martial arts.

forearm (FOR-arm)
The part of the human
arm between the elbow
and the wrist.

gi (GHEE)
A person's life energy.

grain (GRAYN)
The arrangement of fibers
in wood.

hanja (HAHN-juh)
A Korean system of writing
based on borrowed or
modified Chinese characters.

impact (IM-pakt)
A hit with force.

logo (LOH-goh)
An identifying symbol
or motto.

meditation
(meh-dih-TAY-shun)
Where an individual trains
their mind to get a level of
inner thought which gives
them some benefit.

national sport
(NASH-nul SPORT)
A sport or game that is
considered to be a part of the
culture of a nation.

occupied (AH-kyuh-pyd)
Taken and held by enemy troops.

pattern (PA-turn)
A set of basic martial arts movements, mainly defense and attack, done in a sequence to deal with one or more imaginary opponents.

solar plexus (SOH-ler PLEK-sus)
The general area of the stomach below the breastbone.

sparring (SPAR-ing)
A form of training common to many martial arts where you practice skills against an opponent.

stance (STANS)
Way of standing.

unison (YU-nih-sin)
Doing something in exactly the same way at the same time as others.

Websites

Due to the changing nature of Internet links, PowerKids Press has developed an online list of websites related to the subject of this book. This site is updated regularly. Please use this link to access the list:
www.powerkidslinks.com/akgma/tkd/

Read More

Falk, Laine. *Let's Talk Tae Kwon Do.* Scholastic News Nonfiction Readers. Danbury, CT: Children's Press, 2009.

Pawlett, Mark, and Ray Pawlett. *The Tae Kwon Do Handbook.* Martial Arts. New York: Rosen Publishing, 2008.

Wells, Garrison. *Tae Kwon Do: Korean Foot and Fist Combat.* Martial Arts Sports Zone. Minneapolis, MN: Lerner Publishing Group, 2012.

Index